ME, A FLIGHTLESS BIRD

BETTER DEATH THAN A LIFETIME OF LONELINESS

DAVID T NICHOLAS

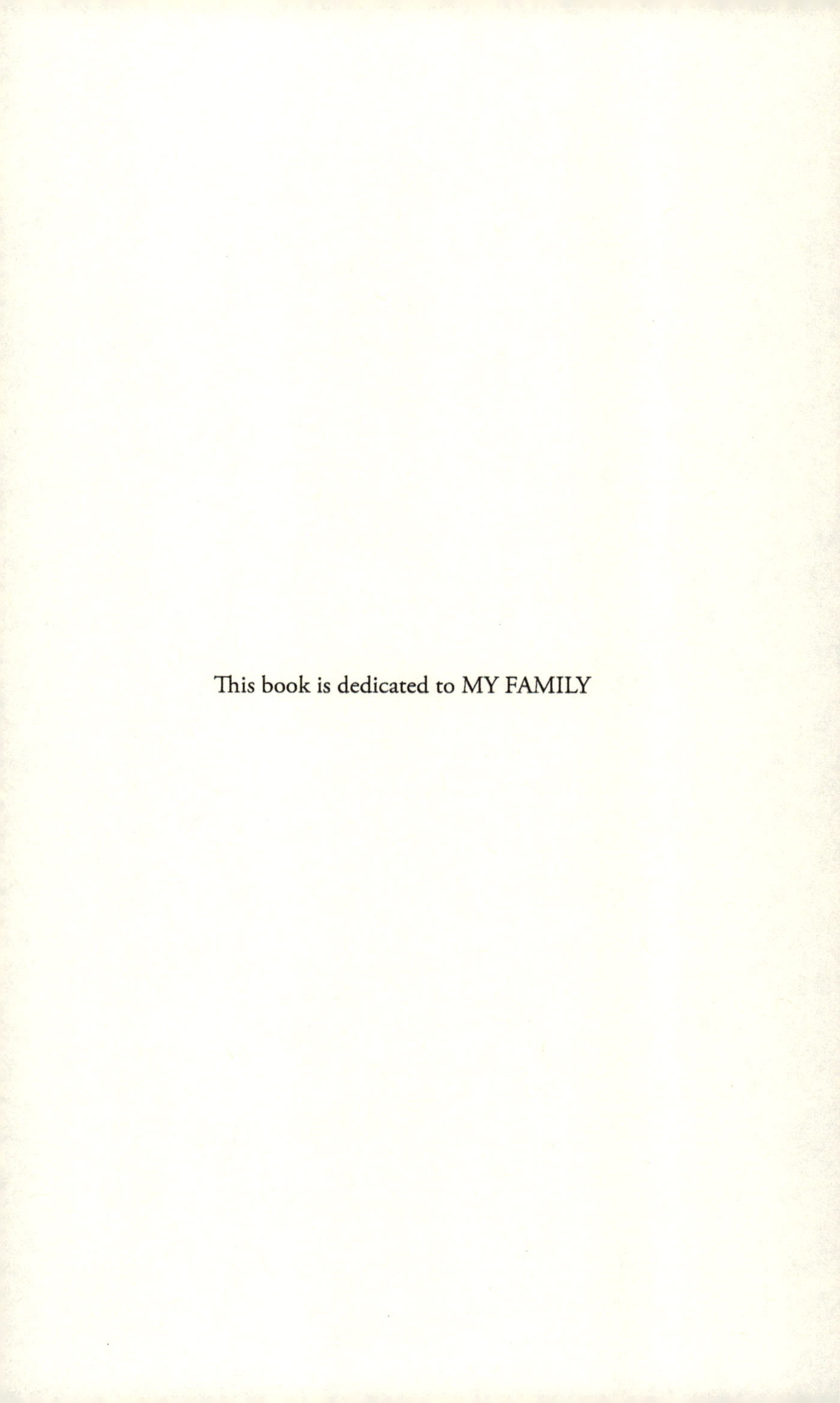

This book is dedicated to MY FAMILY

Contents

Contents

Contents

1. A scruple of love

A scruple of love
I long for
A scruple of love
I crave for
A scruple of love
I ask from you
Be kind to me and grant me
A scruple of love
I ask from you
Just as all Immortal lovers do.

2. The Enchanted Night

The Enchanted Night
All black and white
Deep dark frightened thoughts
Not anyone's delight
Tales of sprits affright
In haunted mansions
Mortal beings living and dead
In mountains, waters and willows
More shuddery even under pillows
The Enchanted Night
All black and white
Deep dark frightened thoughts
Not anyone's delight

3. I lay upon a barren ground

I lay upon a barren ground
And heard voice as that of a murmuring crowd
Of voices dead and decay, fresh and awake
As if the lifeless had more life
And to give more to life
Than life can give life itself.
If you do not believe me its fine
Whenever you get sometime.
Lay upon a barren ground
To feel and hear thoughts as mine.

4. Put these thoughts at rest

The moon is awake
And the sun asleep.
The sun awakes
The moon goes to rest
Perhaps both don't meet for the best
At times we must learn to accept
That the one, the cause
For a broken heart and unsound mind
Are meant to be apart
Just as the sun and the moon
Are always meant to be apart
Perhaps both don't meet for the best
At times we must learn to accept
And best to put these thoughts at rest.

5. Tarry a while longer

Tarry a while longer
I said to my love
As I felt the bond between us stronger
At times in life
Even for ones that we love
Even for ones near and dear
We are so occupied that
Leisure serves us not
To with them in time
Or repay them in kind
What aging life we seek
Where we forget
That someone we love
Or some who is near and dear
Will do the same to us
Wherein their leisure serves them not
To be with you its just a painful thought.

6. I pray you, love me now

I pray you, love me now
As you loved me then
If so, then let not your love in gratis
Name the price
Of which our togetherness be an endless status.
I pray you
Think before you answer
For my love for you is true
It knows not of boundaries
Nor depth
But endless ways to love you
Of ones you never dreamt
Of ones you never felt
All belongs to you
Upon seeing you always my heart does melt .

7. You are my blacksmith

You are my blacksmith
I am the metal
Upon seeing you
My heart does melt
For natural occurrences of smelting
Mould me to love you
Mould me to be with you
Mould me that I am yours
So that I never be another's
For you are my blacksmith
That makes my heart melt.

8. Me; a flightless bird

•8•

I wander like a flightless bird
That once knew to fly and now couldn't.
Wings not clipped but yet I can't
Webbed feet but yet I drown
My flock with me yet I alone
Migration for me every breath I take
Thoughts of me hatched a mistake
To life and life, itself
There is a lot for me at stake
For everyone proud I want to make
Those that cared and even forsake
Me into a worthless, lifeless, flightless bird.
Will I ever fly again ME; a flightless bird
Soar high up in the sky above from self-demur

9. BE

• 9 •

All that I can be
All that will be
All that I wanted to be .
It never really matters to Be.
Be For all to see
I can't be.
Be For all to will
I can't say I will be.
For all that I wanted to be
Maybe I cannot be .
For what I be I'll be
True to myself I'll be
For that's is what I'll be
Then now and ever I'll be
The one, that life choses me to be.

10. A battle called LIFE

Creepy thoughts and creepy plots
Darken the night and darken the thoughts.
Every day and every night
We fight against we fight for right
For all that we have been through
For all that we are going through
For all that we will be through
A life we never asked for
A death we never expected
Its you against the world
In a battle called LIFE
And the end result called DEATH

11. Cities Green, Country Clean

Cities green, country clean
I wish all citizens had visions so keen.
Undo somethings we've done
Undo somethings we've known
Depth of the oceans un measured
Heights of the mountains unknow
Nature less disturbed
Nature less predicted
Let nature take its course
In favour of the living of course
Let animals lost be found
Let nature be the most
Loved and heard musical sound.
For may be then we would have
Cities green, country clean
A Vision accomplished which was so keen.

12. I wonder where is this life taking me

The blind can see me suffering
Yet not the sighted.
The Deaf can see me Crying
Yet not the Hearing.
The Dumb for me they speak
Yet not the unmute
The handless give a helping hand
The limbless walk with me
I wonder where is this life taking me
Or what are the things
I'm yet to hear and see
Of everyone forgetting US and WE
It's just I, ME and MYSELF
In this world for all you see.

13. In love there is nothing wrong

Tell me where my lover walks?
So that I may walk along.
Tell me where my lover flies?
So that I may fly along.
Tell me where my loved one sails?
So that I may sail along.
In doing so there is nothing wrong
For all I long is to love and be loved.
I know not how, where and when
I'll tread upon the one I love
I pray that when that moment comes
I'll walk along ,fly along and sail along
For I know doing so in love there is nothing wrong

14. Thoughts about her doesn't bother me anymore

Now that she lays six feet down below
Must I bend over and kiss her burial
Must I morn that she is gone
For I now posses the heart that loved her
Now that heart is stone
For I know now she lies alone
For when alive was with other
Except me
I guess its best she is alone
And the thought
that she'll be with someone
doesn't bother me any more

15. Enrobe my life

Enrobe my life with that of my dreams
Where fortune, romance, and life;
Stand a better chance than the realism.
Where togetherness stands a better chance
Rather than this lonely realness that I breathe.
Where Love has a place for me
Rather than this destituted one.
Where life has color, meaning, and purpose
Rather than being bitten in the dust.
The hatred I loath
Upon this mortifying self
For being a melancholy bait
To the darkness and pain
Stained by loneliness and heartache
Is there anything else from me?
That this life of mine can drain.
So, Enrobe my life with that of my dreams
Where fortune, romance, and life;
Stand a better chance than the realism.

16. Ups and Downs

Is this life I'm asked to live
A life of ups and downs
Where the ups are less high
And the downs too deep.
Where if others would drown,
And to live life restrain.
I live life with a lot of pain
With nothing left to gain.
Strife, sorrow and suffering
Has been all of my life's bearing
Somethings I would never render
so painful for my heart so tender.

17. Oho! Life of mine

This life of mine I can't restrain
Have learned to live it with pain
What's becoming of me is quite insane
Over the years it's hard to tell
What really caused me the bane.
Gods using me as ane
To see what mankind can go as pain
I'd rather chose to Abstain
But my heart is all just blain
This much I want to know why
So deep inside I'm Elan
To know why this life, I bore
To others it looks so feign,
Coz I do, but deep inside the me is just wane
God when created me was Birdbrain.

18. I'm not all this world needs

I'm not all this world needs
Or is it just to say that I'm not at all needed
with a purpose left to live
and the purpose becomes lifeless
with no one to love or care
to be loved or to be cared for
this life I live is not what I need
this life i live is not what I've asked for
this life I live is not for anyone to live
I silently want this life of mine to be over
if the life I want isn't mine
I don't want to live a life some else planned for me
a life of suffering , misery , agony and all the synonyms
of the word pain in its worst form of life
just dwell deep within me
others are so blinded that they can't see
This life of mine I don't need If this world really needs me not
for I am not all this world needs
and I am not needed in this world .

19. DO

If your Done doing what you do
Then do what you have to be get doing.
if you are doing what you have done
Stop and do something that has to be done.
Don't say you have done all your work
because if you have really done; then your really done .
For in life you have to do alot
And there is alot of work for you and me to be done
We are really done ,
only when life is really done with us .

20. Don't bother

Don't bother
About me I'm not ok
Don't bother
About me I'm not well
Don't bother
About me the work I'm doing is not paying off
Don't bother
About me I'm not sleeping well
Don't bother
About me I'm not my self
Don't bother
About me no one does
Don't bother
About me no one calls me
Don't bother
About me no one messages me
Don't bother
About me you never really did
Not that it will make a difference
But just that you should know
Your way better than me in everysingle way
Thank you so much for not caring even a single day .

21. Make what you want of my words

Make what you want of my words
Of which I have said in my past
Or talking to you at present
Of what I am to speak to you in the future
But just remember maketh quick
For all the words that I speak off
Will soon be just words from my past
When I am gone far away
Where no words will you hear
For I will not be able to say so
Make what you want of my words
Maketh quick , maketh wise
For when I am gone nothing I said
Should come as a surprise .

22. Life's curtains are drawn

When the curtains
To my life are drawn
Surely most would forget
That I was even born
For them my words
Of comfort may not be a thing
But for those that are near and dear
Feel not that I am not here
But wherever my afterlife
Know that I am better than here
This I promise and you know me
If I love and care for someone
I'll never forget and leave them
Even after my death
I'll find ways to watch over
For that is what my life's about.

23. A portrait of my life

I wish I could continue life as it is
Every single day I wake
And like a painter stokes
To finish his work
I try to paint my own life
Upon a canvas of life
where the portrait of my life
Has been painted wherein
Pain, misery, and agony follow
and, my life continues again without
A glitch that sleeps brings within.
For when the painter had finished
A portrait of my life
A Masterpiece indeed
Of a hidden sequestered life
Of loneliness, wretchedness, unfortunate life
Maybe the artist the DEVIL
Maybe the artist GOD
Or Maybe the painter of life
Whomsoever it is; has to pay the price
For the portrait of an ill-fated life.

24. I'm not all this world needs

I'm not all this world needs
Or is it just to say that I'm not at all needed
with a purpose left to live
and the purpose becomes lifeless
with no one to love or care
to be loved or to be cared for
this life I live is not what I need
this life I live is not what I've asked for
this life I live is not for anyone to live
I silently want this life of mine to be over
if the life I want isn't mine
I don't want to live a life someone else planned for me
A life of suffering, misery, agony, and all the synonyms
Of the word pain in its worst form of life
Just dwell deep within me
Others are so blinded that they can't see
This life of mine I don't need
For I am not all this world needs
And I am not needed in this world.

25. The destituted Amorist

An Amorist so destituted from love
For his heart with another
Who cared so less listening to her mother
From time to time she likes to
Crush his heart that melts for her
Although with hatred , but loves her more
The pain deep within he does store
Where within there isn't place anymore
But she fills it with dark heartache
Of even which even evil does lack.

26. The waves that hit the shore

If ever you find yourself alone and sad

Or find the need to talk to yourself

Go to the beach and sit ashore

And hear the waves, as they hit the shore

They speak aloud and whisper too

So many lonely tales they tell

Every single time they come ashore

Tales of the sea; of arduous and brave lives

Of seafaring men and women.

Of beings and creatures a subject of moot

Even Of pirates and their vicious loot.

At times they bring afloat the bodies

That drowned or have been killed

By the rough sea or the voyage thru it.

The waves that hit the shore

Every time they come to Ashore

The tales they tell you will never bore

Even of tales that occurred a long, long time ago.

27. An Imaginary Name

Can I blame you for going away
When I was just a little.
Now you are just an imaginary name
With a power that words can't express.
A part of you in me; with me; for me
A blessing in disguise.
life always with or without you
I won't doubt it would have been the same
But I would have preferred the one crafted with you.
There are so many mysterious ways
That we come across in our lifespan
Life's magical and capabilities are Witnessed
we see its many mysterious ways
The mystery of your Absence
Is perhaps The one I would never understand
I hope you always watched down on me
A bleeding life I lead
Clotted in many ways
it's just been carrying on for days
Life's mysterious ways I never will understand
For the mysterious way of life
Will always be mysterious for me and everyone around.

28. The Journey of my Life

The station was Earth

The platform was my country

The train was my life

If you didn't board it or

If you didn't take the journey with me

That means You missed An opportunity of a lifetime,

The opportunity to experience All the emotions of life

An opportunity to see the real me

The compartments in the train

Were filled with a lifetime

Full of experience you can't imagine

To continue the journey from where we met

Will be difficult from where I'm now

The train stopped at many places

It had new changes

Met a lot of wonderful and horrible things

Just want you to know

If you didn't board it or

If you did take the journey with me

That means You missed an opportunity of a lifetime.

29. Beauty upon a barren tree

I came upon a barren tree
Which was once as flamboyant As can be
It's been ages since
new leaves grew since a bud formed
Or a flower bloom nor did a fruit ripen
Abandoned for ages now
Beauty lost and greyish black
Of which once was a colouration
Of many different colours during the years
No one really know the cause
for the macabre of the barren tree.
The artist wonderd how
But could never really tell
When suddenly She noticed
Upon the long lost barren tree
Pearched a Macaw
In splits of a second the ambit
Caused by the conjointly of the two
A picturesque together of its beauty
Did the artist capture
Of the bird and the barren tree
As if the both together were meant to be.

As if the barren tree
Was waiting for the bird to be pearch upon
It's tree trunk and barks
For the life that was Lifeless
Gained life and remained
As a portrait of life
Within the artist
And the one who possessed it.
The beauty upon a barren tree
Is something for everyone to see
For Everyone who looks at the potrait
Looks at it in veneration.

30. This lonely life

It's only when you come
And i see you
That this lonely life
Of mine gets to
Wear on a smile.
Your presence near me
For that little time
Just can't get enough of you
I can't take my eyes of you
Or can't stop thinking
about you for a second
it's only when you come
and i see you
that this lonely life
of mine gets to
wear on a smile.

31. Drowned

If all is found
And nothing is lost
If all is lost
And nothing is found
If all that's found
Is ever drowned
If all that is never found
Is all been drowned
If all our answers
To our questions
Lie deep down the Oceans
Why aren't we drowned
Trying to get all the answers
To our questions
Because we do drown every day
Without being deep down
The Oceans drowning.
Where we don't get answers.

32. Untill life comes to Rest

All our worries in life come
They keep coming just like the
Waves that come ashore
They are never going to stop
They will be calm, arrogant
Terror, high and low
They are never going to Stop
Until life come to Rest.
On that day some
Of us do not long
But some whose life
Is full of misery and troubles
Hardships and never-ending
Disheartened and loved-less
Like mine, they wish upon
Life to come to Rest.

33. One night awaits everyone

One night awaits everyone
Silent, dark, and peaceful
Cold, numb, and eternal rest
For once the eyes are shut
It's like the night That
One night awaits everyone.
it's a night that forbids the light
it's a night that forbids life
and it that one night everyone is aware
the One night that awaits everyone.

34. The beginnings of all things are small

The beginnings of all things are small
Just as life begins small
In a mother's womb.

The beginnings of all things are small
Just as the tiny seed
Springs into a big tree.

The beginnings of all things are small
Just like the drops of water
Before a heavy shower.

The beginnings of all things are small
Just as a baby girl grows into a teen
Then a woman becomes a mother.

The beginnings of all things are small
Just as a baby boy grows into a teen
Then a man becomes a father.

The beginnings of all things are small
Just as an Alphabet becomes a word

Then becomes a sentence in a poem or a book.

35. Careless

A Careless merchant, a future beggar.

A Careless mind, double work.

A careless husband is a divorced one.

A careless wife a reckless life.

A careless mother is a heartless one.

A careless father is a ruined family.

A careless Daughter hapless motherhood.

A careless Son hapless fatherhood.

A Careless brother unpredictable family.

A Careless sister lack motherhood qualities.

A Careless Teacher an uncertain future.

A Careless student with an ambivalent and vexed life.

A careless leader a pointless nation.

A careless cook insipid broth.

A careless laborer causes unimaginable peril.

A careless Employee seeks unimaginable tsuris.

A careless neighbor is a thief's delight.

A careless self a reckless and unimaginable life.

36. Dream, dream, dream

Dream, dream, dream
Of all that you want
There is a dream for you
And a dream for me
There is a dream for everyone
A life filled with dreams
When asleep and awake
But never be disquieted
If they are to be Foiled
For not all dreams come true
And not all reality are dreams.

37. Treasured things

We like to treasure
A lot of things in life.
It may be one,
Maybe two,
Or whose to know
Maybe more.
We can treasure
All the things
We want in life,
But the most important thing
That we all must treasure
Is life and life itself

38. Never forget

Never forget the one
That held your hand
Never forget the one
That is holding your hand
Never forget the one
Hand that cooks for you
Never forget the one
Hand that is cooking you
Never forget the one
Hand that feeds you
Never forget the one
Hand that is feeding you
Never forget the one
Hand That bathed you
Never forget the one
Hand That is bathing you
Never forget the one
Hand that Clothed you
Never forget the one
Hand that is Clothing you
Never forget the one
Hand that looked after you
Never forget the one

Hand that is looking after you
Never forget the one
Hand that thought you
Never forget the one
Hand that is teaching you
it's not that they wanted anything in return
But they definitely
Don't deserve to be forgotten.
They deserve a little gratitude
And remembrance in some little way.
For the very thought of never forgetting them
pays for all the little sacrifices
That they have done for you in life.

39. A word called mother

• 42 •

A word called mother
The word that is Synonymous
With the word sacrifice
For All that she does
Is just a selfless act
For her children and loved ones
we want to give her the world
But to her, we are her world.

40. The Queue

The queue we have at times
What loss of time in
One short span of life
There is nothing one can do about
But the person who just makes us wait
Can see that he speeds up the queue
Or have an organized waiting place
Where worry less and patience grow
So we don't mind if
we have to wait again tomorrow
But no one cares about you
Especially if you're waiting in a queue
You need something you got to wait
If not march out if the que
Find your way home most would say
The time we take waiting at places
Is almost one-fourth of our lifetime
Save a fraction of your life
and the lives of others
By Organizing a proper Queue
When Approached Ensure you moil
Your duties at hand to reduce the Queue
Or when in one be well organized and brisk.

41. A forgotten lad

I was in love
I always wanted to be,
To be in someone's heart
And be held in one's arms
Be in their mind and never begotten
Life takes another turn
For me and nothing did I learn
Pain, grief and suffering I earn
No one's heart, no one's arms
In no one's mind
Perhaps never loved at all
Or even if falsely did get loved
Each and every time I fall in love
I'm just another forgotten lad.

42. Bloom where you are planted

Bloom where you are planted
learn to live and survive life
Wherever you are or
Whatever situation you are in.
learn to spreads your branches
flowers, and fruits all over
but remember that your roots
have to firm to the ground
even better if its firm ground
to the place from where it sprung
and the place once bloomed from
So, bloom where you're planted
learn to live and survive life
Wherever you are or
Whatever situation you are in.

43. Walking Alone

There's a lot of difference
When we are walking alone
And walking
With someone by our side.
Especially walking
With the one we love
Every step that we take
Is carefully watched over.
Ensuring the walk we have
Is a safe and guided walk.
A feeling or something
We would never Experience
Walking Alone.

When we see everyone
Walking with someone,
And we are walking alone
It saddens your heart.
What's worse is when you lose
The one you truly love
And have to take
The walk of life all alone.
Then you realize the real difference

And the real pain of walking
With somebody by your side
And walking alone.

44. Memories

If today is gone
It will never come back
But the memories
We make today
Can be the memories
We have for life
So make them count
Decide what are the memories
That you want to have
For the rest of your life.
The deeds that you do today
Irrespective of good or bad
Will definitely come back to you
If you couldn't make a difference
In the world yesterday
Try to make it today
So you'll be remembered tomorrow
Life is a collection of memories
Of yesterday and today for tomorrow
If you're wise you'll understand
If not, time will speak for itself.

45. There is a time for all

There is a time for all

A time to rise

A time to fall

A time to trust

A time to doubt

A time to be an optimist

A time to be a Pessimist

A time to love

A time to have

A time to sleep

A time to be awake

A time to live

A time to die

A time for you

A time for me

A time for us

And there is a time for us All.

46. Priceless

There are alot of things in this world
That are priceless to you and me
But there are things
That are priceless for everyone
A mother's love
A father's care
A protective brother
A sister's affection
The bond of friendship
The togetherness of a family
When you're loved one
Stands up for you against the world
The warmth of a blanket
The hand that feeds us
The early morning sun
The quiet and peaceful moon
A good day's work
A good night's sleep
God's blessings and love
And the thought
That God is watching us Always
These are really priceless
If you experienced it you will agree

There is no harm in you disagreeing
Because life is never the same For us all
we all have the right
To believe in what's priceless
For us and what's not .

47. If God is silent

If god is silent
Then what does it mean.
After all the prayers
And tears within
In silence I did it all .
Must I be loud and make noise ,
Shout and sing his name
For him to speak with me.
I know not the plans of God
I even desire not to
But would deeply want to know
After all that is happening on this Earth
And my life's Bereft.
If god is silent
Then what does it mean.

48. In my life

In my life
I've never heard the words
That I want to hear .

In my life
I've never seen the things
That I wanted to see .

In my life
I've never smell the things
That I wanted to smell .

In my life
I've never spoken the words
That I really want to speak.

In my life
I've never been helped
The way I wanted to be .

In my life
I live like someone
Who never wants to be .

In my life
I regret that no one is
There for me like I've been for others .

In my life
The one who knows me is God
And if he is always silent
So it's justified that the rest of the world is.

49. The shadow of love

The shadow of love
Will never depart once upon
Till death may be ,
If love so stong or bitter
Might follow your soul within
Such is the shadow of love

The shadow of love
Does follow everyone thou
It really doesn't matter who you are
Unlike the shadow that follows us
It prefers to remain within us
Such is the shadow of love.

50. Life's deplorable

If love is the only best thing
In this world of ours
Then it's obviously even the worst.
Would I bury the broken love I had
Yes, I would and I wouldn't
For a love so true, would have.
Thought of both abdication
Of my feelings deep inside
I wish someone, be an imitator
Of my life to see
What I've gone through
But it isn't the way
Life is, it's mostly I must
Say deplorable.

51. If ever there is someone

If ever there is someone
To love me now
I guess they have
To look for me six feet below
I ain't going to the skies above
For if my heart
should break again
I would never
Be able to bear the fall
Even after death's call
So I prefer to lie six feet down
To avoid the fall the thousandth time.

52. A Book Fair

A noisy, busy, yet a quiet place
The noise is not outward
But one's heavy inward thoughts
Of what to choose and What not to.

what can be read and what cannot
Most come in with a choice of fixed reads
some come to see the cheapy reads
some the attractive illustrations for kids.

some come to add books to their collection.
A book fair I must say is a place of grace.
But What's the point of going to a book fair
When poetry isn't treated fair.

Is it really that you don't care
Or is it really the fare
For some books might be a nightmare
But there are those that really care .

Some know what they like and want
Some don't know what they like and want
Know that whatever book you choose

is a choice of yours and it's completely fair.

But don't leave poetry unnoticed it's completely unfair
Just stand stop and stare
so that poetry may gain some love at the fair.
And poems may gain some lover's affairs
Apart from those nasty snarls and stares.

53. Difficult things to say

Some things are really difficult to say
As the things, I say below
Whether the night is beautiful or the day
Is the sun more useful than the moon
Is life really better than the afterlife
If love is a cure for all emotions
Or if laughter is really the best medicine
Is god always watching us
Does he really care about anyone
Living creature upon this Earth
Or is mankind left to fend for themselves
The surety of the beginning and end of life .
These are difficult things to say
You may or may not think my way
Maybe when you're wise enough
You know that these are things
That matter to us in life
And these are really difficult things to say .

54. Thoughts in your head

At night the thoughts in your head
Run wild and free.
The thought and word process
Different from the day.
The words tend to break off
From that forgetful strain, stress
An unthinkable day.
And you walk freely during the night
For the thoughts in your head
Have calmed down and put to rest
While you are fast asleep
Dreaming about everything
But not the deep thoughts in your head
That ran during the day.

55. The places in my head

No matter the place I stay
No matter the places I vist
No matter how beautiful it is
I would always love the places
Ive imagined in my head

No matter what I'm thought
No matter what I read
No matter how beautiful whatever I read is
I would always love the thoughts
I've imagined in my head

No matter how beautiful my life is
No matter who I'm with in reality
No matter even if i had the best life
I would always love the life
Ive imagined in my dreams.

56. Priceless

There are alot of things in this world
That are priceless to you and me
But there are things
That are priceless for everyone
A mother's love
A father's care
A protective brother
A sister's affection
The bond of friendship
The togetherness of a family
When you're loved one
Stands up for you against the world
The warmth of a blanket
The hand that feeds us
The early morning sun
The quiet and peaceful moon
A good day's work
A good night's sleep
God's blessings and love
And the thought
That God is watching us Always
These are really priceless
If you experienced it you will agree

There is no harm in you disagreeing
Because life is never the same For us all
we all have the right
To believe in what's priceless
For us and what's not.

57. To life and life alone

This world is not yours .
Neither is this world mine .
This world is yours
As long as have life in you .
This world is mine
As long as I have life in me .
Once the life we have in us is gone
So is the ain of life
That is the life we owned
Comes to an end.
Life is rich as long as you have it ,
Once gone it all remains
For the ones who have life in them
So this world neither
belongs to you or me
It belongs to life and life alone .

58. Circle of Life

The circle of life
It has no beginning and end .
No one knows how it began
No one knows how it will end
But it's sure we know
All things good and bad about it
What we should,
And What we shouldn't
What we must,
And what we mustn't.
We must know that there
Is nothing more precious and sacred
Than the circle of life.
It must lived and passed on
For Eternity and sacrosanct
Is that of The circle of life .

59. love is like the moon

Love is like the moon
It keeps changing every day
But it will remain
And be called the same
it will come and go
But never vanish completely
those that embrace it
during its changing phases
shall be rewarded when
it is fully bright and illuminated

60. Will i ever find someone

If I ever love someone
Will they love me back the same
Or if they don't love me as I do
Do I solely have myself to blame
Even after telling the world their name
Will, i ever find someone
Who would love me just the same
Just the way I love them
And shout to the world
Feeling proud
With my name alongside theirs.
Will, i ever find someone,
Tell me will I ever find someone.

61. Walk of life

The walk of life may vary
From person to person
From second to second
From minute to minute
From hour to hour
From day to day
From month to month
From year to year
But one thing is true and common
About the walk of life
That as it began so must it end
The time taken from life to life may vary
But the walk of life must eventually end

62. US

Me and you
We make us

He and she
with me makes us

them and they,
I along make us.

we and them
together makes us.

when more than one
and all together it makes us.